SHENANIGANS

DON WISDOM

NEWMAN SPRINGS PUBLISHING
320 Broad Street
Red Bank, NJ 07701

First originally published by Newman Springs Publishing 2020

ISBN 978-1-64801-751-3 (Paperback)
ISBN 978-1-64801-752-0 (Digital)

Printed in the United States of America

INTRODUCTION

My attempt to write this little book is not to write a story like a novel. It is just a gathering of memories taken from my life. I have no idea if these memories are correct or not, but it shouldn't matter. It is meant to be a fun read. You may find poor punctuation, misspelled words, and other errors, even spacing errors. My only hope is this book can bring some joy to some of you.

1

THE EARLY EARLY YEARS

When I was a wee little lad, I didn't like to go to bed, evidently because dear old Dad and Mom had to load me in the car and go for a short drive. This drive was usually about one or two trips around the block, and then I was sound asleep and they could put me to bed.

A few months later, when I could zip around the house at the super speed of a slow crawl, I tried something different. With all those months of knowledge behind me, I became very intelligent and found out I could hide behind the couch, and no one could find me. At least, that is what I thought. So I would crawl back there with my head hidden and think I was safe. What I didn't know was that my back end was still out in plain sight. Everybody could see me. Moral of this story: Cover your butt or watch out for your own rear end!

Time moved on, and when it came time to really start learning things, I ran into a snag. I found out that I had a big sister. I knew there were other beings in the house. I knew who Mom was. That was very important, but I didn't know what a sister and a brother were. There was one of each in the household I grew up in.

Big sister tried to help me with many things. I don't know what big brother did; probably what big brothers do best—make my young life miserable. Anyway, I was supposed to learn how to tie my shoestrings, but that was hard. I would try and try until I would give up and go running to big sister with that look that would turn any hard heart to putty. "Sister, sister," I would whine, "tie my shoestrings."

She would tie my shoestrings, but sometimes Mom would interfere. Moms do that sometimes, you know. This is what I would hear: *"Hazel, leave the boy alone! He will never learn to tie his shoestrings with you helping him all the time!"* You know, to this day, I wear slip-on shoes or use Velcro.

Big brother wasn't all bad either. He would let me run around with him and his friends. I liked going places with him and his friends. After all, they were about three years older than I was and very mature. Once in a while, Mom would make me stay home. She would say silly things, like, "Your brother needs some time with his friends without you tagging along." I thought I was an important part of that group. Guess not!

One time, Dad told me to water the lawn by hand instead of using the sprinkler, and then he left. The lawn had a lot of sand in it, and the water would just disappear. Dad came back and got after me and made me water some more. By then, I was not a happy camper.

Big brother comes along and mocked me. "I told you to water that lawn, now get out there and do what I told you!"

I hit him with the hose. He took it away from me, and the fight was on. By the way, I never won any of those. After all, he was three years my senior. Dad got after both of us. Mom got after Dad. She told him I did water the lawn for a long time. Brother got in trouble for teasing me, and I walked away a free child! That was a good day!

For a while, we lived on two-and-a-half acres, just outside the city limits. My big brother and I were out in the pasture, chasing this big fish up and down the ditch. I backed into the electric fence, and it knocked me on my backside. Brother thought it was funny. There goes that business with the back end again. That wasn't my only run-in with an electric fence. We were fishing one time and came upon (you guessed it) an electric fence. My brother stepped over it, and I tried. Didn't make it. Once again, on my backside.

Not all my time around an electric fence was bad, though. We had a dog named Stubb. He liked to chase sticks or just about anything you could throw. I would throw the stick under the fence, and he would go after it. He would yip going after the stick and yip bringing it back. I must have laughed at that dog for fifteen minutes, listening to him go, "Yip, yip, yip!"

Oh! I almost forgot. Picture this fishing trip. Out to a farm pond filled with fish, we went a fishing in the springtime, and the magpies were nesting. For those of you who may not know what a magpie is, they are a black and white bird that is as noisy as a crow. They can be a bit cranky, especially in the springtime when you get too close to their nest. We got too close. They began to chase us.

We jumped on our bikes, and away we went. Remember, I ran around with older boys. They were way ahead of me, and the magpies were closing fast. I was peddling as fast as my little legs would go, but that wasn't fast enough. The magpies started divebombing me, and I almost fell off my bike. There are disadvantages of running around with older boys.

I have another fishing story for you. When I was around eighteen or nineteen, my older brother and I went fishing. We took his pickup, and when we were in the mountains, up on the Boise front, he told me to watch the creek for a place to fish. So being kind of smart-mouthed like boys can be, I said, "Turn here." There was no road there, but he turned, and down over the embankment we went, right down to the water, and we went fishing. I don't want to say that little trip frightened me, but he had been fishing about ten minutes before I could walk again. The moral of this story is: Don't tell someone to turn unless there is a road there.

Another time, we were out driving around in his pickup, and my mouth got me in trouble again. I liked to cry and whine, just to give him a bad time, so I was moaning about his driving. If any of you remember, those older cars had this steering wheel with a silver ring in the middle of it. When he finally got tired of my whining, he pulled that silver ring off the steering wheel, handed it to me, and said, "You drive."

Once again, I wished I had a spare pair of blue jeans with me!

Did you know that night crawlers would rather dig in the ground than to go fishing? I put this one worm on my hook and tossed it in into the deep blue. He crawled off the hook, up the line, through the eyeholes on the fishing pole, up my arm, to my shoulder, and jumped up on my nose, looked me in the eye, and said, "I am not going fishing. Put me back in the ground." I don't fish with live bait any more.

THE TREE

This is one of those times when my brother would tease me till I was ready to fight. He would get me to that point and then bolt and run. He never ran because he was afraid of me. He ran because it was funny to him. He knew I couldn't catch him. Out the door he would go, and then he would jump and grab a limb and swing up into a tree. There he would sit and laugh at me. I didn't know how to get up the tree and I couldn't reach the limb. Sometimes when in need, the answer comes to us. Finally, one day, I had him treed. I ran out into the street and grabbed two handfuls of gravel and proceeded to throw rocks at him. He never ran up the tree anymore.

We were getting older now. Sis was gone, all grown up, leaving my brother and myself home with the parents. Big brother was learning to smoke cigarettes by then. Trouble was coming.

Dad and Mom left the house for just a little while. Big brother decided to take one or two of Dad's smokes and headed for the basement—not a good move. They came home, and Dad smelled the smoke and the sulfur from the matches. What's sulfur anyway? I had never heard of such a thing. So Dad came downstairs (nowhere to run). *Here it comes.* "Okay, who's smoking?"

No answer.

"If I don't find out who is smoking, both of you get a spanking!"

Dad already knew who it was, but he got no answer. We both got a spanking. I told my brother, "I am not doing that again for you. Next time, you are on your own."

He was pretty nice to me for a while.

THE ACCIDENT

Sometimes we would ride our bikes to grade school. Down the block we would go, across the busy street, and into a subdivision.

From there, we would ride through the subdivision to another busy street. The subdivision would gain altitude until you reached the far end of it, so you found four high walls blocking the view of the road. I was there first, and as I started down the hill, I looked back and shouted, "Watch this!"

I hear this: "I wouldn't do that if I were you!"

Too late. I was on my way. I crossed the intersection, and broadside, a car came down the hill. The impact threw me over the car into the upcoming traffic lane, and I landed on my back. The car went to the bottom of the hill before he got it stopped. He backed up the hill to see if I was all right. I was fine, nothing hurt, but my bike was broken. I couldn't ride it.

I had to carry it the rest of the way to school. Good advice from my bother. Not my finest hour. I managed to have a mental block while in school, and after school, I raced out the door and jumped on my bike. It went nowhere, and I fell flat on my face. I had to drag it home. Meanwhile, my brother rode his bike home, and by the time I got there, Dad and Mom knew what happened. I walked to school the rest of the year. I didn't know how long it was until I had another bike, but it seemed like an eternity.

JUNIOR HIGH

First day of school. Homeroom. Roll call. The teacher was going through roll call, trying to get to know the new flock of students. It went something like this:

"May Johnson?"

"Here."

"Bill Bennet?"

"Yo."

And the list went on at a fast pace. And then came my name.
"Here!"

Long pause.

"Question, are you Montie's brother?"

"Yes!" Pause.

"Oh no! You are even sitting where he sat."

9

It seems big brother has a reputation. The next day, we had a new homeroom teacher. Strange, don't you think? Big brother wasn't a troublemaker, but he did get into a few fights across the street. No life as I see it!

EARLY CHILDHOOD

I remember getting upset with my mom one time. You know how frustrating parents can be. Anyway, I was going to show her, so I ran away from home. I realize now that parents are a necessary element in a child's life.

Where we lived then had a small irrigation ditch that ran across the front of the property and down one side. We had a small bridge across the ditch on the side for the car to drive and park in the back. So being super-intelligent, I ran away and hid under the bridge, not knowing I didn't even leave the property. *I will show her. She won't find me.*

She didn't even look for me. After what I thought was a long time, I came home and greeted Mom like this: "Hi, Mom, I am home."

She replied, "I didn't know you were gone! You been hiding under the bridge again? Want a sandwich? Your favorite, peanut butter and jelly." Life was good again. Balance was back in place.

Moms are great people, but they are a bit mysterious. Did you know they have eyes in the back of their heads? My brother and I couldn't get away with anything. She always knew. At least, that is what we thought. We would do what boys do and we would hear Mom: "You boys stop that. Don't make me come in there."

How did she know? We found out too late. We were adults before we knew that secret. When you are doing something you are not supposed to be doing, be sure and be noisy. That's the secret. When you are not noisy is when she knows you are up to no good.

Mom's know just about everything! My mom knew what I liked in my lunch for school. If she sent a meat sandwich, it either came back or was exchanged for (guess what) peanut butter and jelly.

Mom was good at many things. She would bake a pie and put it in a window to cool. We would steal it, and I think maybe we only ate one. The price was too high. She had her ways of dealing with us. When we got too far out of line, we ended up doing dishes for two weeks or scrubbing floors. Any way you look at it, the price was too high. If we really got out of line and she couldn't control us, she would go to the ultimate weapon. This is what she would do, and it never failed.

"You boys stop it right now or you dad will deal with you when he gets home."

He always dealt with us! I don't know how it was for my brother, but for me, the worst punishment was waiting for him to get home. He was a concrete finisher, so he didn't have regular hours. You could wait for ten minutes or ten hours.

I remember the good things mom Did also. Things like the pies and the warm white or yellow cake with the warm vanilla pudding just waiting for us after school. There was also the leftover pie crust with cinnamon and sugar on it. Once there was a whole bowl of popcorn sitting on the table when I came home from school. No one was home, so I sat down and ate the whole thing. When the family came home, there was a question. "Where is all the popcorn?"

Now I am not very smart, so I replied, "I ate it."

Wrong answer! Reply was, "That was for all of us."

My answer? "I didn't know." Again, wrong answer. I don't even know what my punishment was, but I am sure there was one.

Sometimes parents are hard to understand. Once I watched Mom knitting something, so I asked, "What are you making?"

"Cat for to make kitten britches," was her answer. To this day, I have no idea what that means.

Let's look at Dad for a while. My parents were not mean to us, but they were authority figures to me. I would want to ask Dad for something but I was afraid he would say no, so I would go to Mom. She would never answer for him. I would get things like, "You will have to ask him" or "He can't say yes if you don't ask him."

One time, I did ask, and he answered like I thought he would. I wanted to go to a school football game. I had a car, but the drive up was about two hours, and it would be dark on the drive back. He said no, and I was upset with him, but he didn't know it. You didn't tell Dad when you were mad at him.

Dad took my brother and I out back and showed us a stack of lumber from the concrete forms he built. This is how it went. Dad speaking, "I want you boys to separate the two-by-fours from the two-by-eights and the other lumber. See all those nails? Take them out of the lumber. Straighten them out so I can use them again. Separate the different sizes and put them over there. Stack the two-by-fours here and the two-by-eights over there and the rest over here. I have to go look at a job, but I will be back."

When he got back, he would check on us. If it wasn't done per his instructions, he didn't get mad or anything. He just tore it all down and scattered it out. He just said, "Do it right this time." And he walked away. Lesson learned. If you do it right the first time, you don't need to do it again.

Another thing about Dad is this. When you become a young healthy teenager and think you are big and strong, don't take Dad on. Out in the front yard one day, there were maybe four to six of us tough teenagers who were going to take Dad on. We knew we could take him, but he had to rub our confidence in our noses. He said, "Tell you what, I will even lie down on the ground. You get a hold of me how you want and see if you can keep me there. You won't be able to, but you can try. We thought we had it made. It didn't take him long until we were scattered all over the yard, and he was standing above us, saying, "What'd the matter, boys? Can't you handle it?"

We tried two or three more times, and he was right—we couldn't handle it.

I remember once when my brother and I were fighting, and Mom couldn't handle us. She told dad, and he placed us on the couch opposite end of each other. Then he told us, "Sit up straight, look forward, and not a peep out of either of you."

Do you know how hard it is to just sit and look forward and do nothing else? I would rather have gotten a spanking and let go, but no. Dad made us sit there, which seemed like a very long time. After those kinds of episodes, we were good for a while. But it never lasted long. It became business as usual.

Somewhere along the teen years, my brother and I took on different personalities. He took to smoking. I didn't. He took to fighting other boys. I didn't. He took to chasing all the girls he could. I didn't. His life was more interesting than mine.

With that said, he got into more trouble than I did. He grew a reputation. I didn't. You see the pattern here, don't you? His life was vibrant, mine wasn't. Our lives fit each one of us, and we were happy. I should make it clear here. He wasn't a bully. His fights consisted of fighting the bullies for picking on someone weaker than they were.

He still got called to the office when something happened. One time, he was called in, and the principle accused him of some crime he didn't commit. Here is how it went.

Principle: "You were seen doing this and that thing just a few minutes ago."

My brother became unglued a little bit, looked the principle in the eyes, and boldly stated, "I did not do it, *and by God, I can prove it!*" He was standing next to one of the teachers, watching me play tetherball. They called the teacher in, and he verified what my brother said. He walked out a free teenager.

In my last year of junior high, we had a wrestler in the heavyweight class. This kid was just plain big. Not fat, but *big*. He was what I called a gentle giant. Some of the boys liked to tease him. One day, they were after him, and he went for them. They jumped into their VW bug. You know, the one with the engine in the back? He grabbed the back of the VW and lifted it off the ground. At the same time, the driver had the pedal to the metal, but he was going nowhere fast. The gentle giant said, "You better let up on the gas because I am going to drop this car."

They let up on the gas, and he let the car down and walked away. They never bothered him again.

HIGH SCHOOL

I went to high school with a set of twins. Twins can make life very interesting. The teachers never knew which one was in their class. They would ask, but the twins always gave them the right first

13

name. The same holds true for the girls. They never knew which twin they were on a date with. The trials and tribulations of the teenager in the fifties and sixties.

Not too much happened in high school. I was a bashful child, even at the ripe old age of seventeen, eighteen, and nineteen. The girls liked m, but I couldn't talk to them. They were still scary to me. I did like one girl, and she liked me, but one day, I knocked her books out of her hands and walked away without helping to pick them up. I thought that was what boys did when they liked a girl. I was wrong! My love life never got off the ground. The non-existing relationship never happened. Girls can be narrow-minded!

2

THE MILITARY

In the year 1964, the Vietnam war was in full swing. The draft was still in effect, and I was primed to go to war. I knew if I was drafted, I would be in the army and off to the war zone. Now I didn't mind defending my country if asked, but I thought there was a better way. I looked at the navy and said, "No, don't want to spend six months at a time out to sea." The marines was like the army. Not a chance. Didn't want to go there.

For some reason, the Coast Guard didn't even enter my mind. That left the Airforce. Good choice. I spent four years there and came home in one piece. I spent about half the time stateside in basic training and at Travis Air Base in California. The other half was in Greece on the island of Crete. That was good duty, like going on vacation at the government's expense. We had a beach right on the base. Swimming, body surfing, and sunburn were the entertainment of the day when off duty. Of course, we went to town and harassed the locals sometimes, but you didn't want to get in too much trouble over there. You would find yourself confined to base, and that wasn't as much fun.

When I went overseas, I had to fly to the Big Apple first. I had never been east of the Rockies before then, so I flew to New York early. That was a mistake. I took a hotel room downtown and found out I had way too much time on my hands. I went for a walk four or five blocks away from the hotel and found myself real close to being lost. A person can get lost in the big cities just as easy as in the mountains. I began to notice the paint on the buildings was beginning to peel, and the buildings looked rundown and uncared for. That spooked me, so I looked back to the last corner I turned on and began to backtrack.

I did find the hotel, but I was upset, so I bought a bottle of brandy. Now I never drank alcohol before, and a little bit of that stuff goes a long way. I found myself sick the next morning, so I poured the rest of the brandy down the sink and never drank brandy again.

When it was time to leave New York, I was ready to go. I hailed a cab and headed for Kennedy Airport. There was snow on the roads, and the cab driver was driving too fast and bounced off a guard rail. The cabbie said, "I guess I better slow down." But he didn't. Boy, was I glad to get to the airport!

I finally arrived in Greece, landed in Athens, and got on a smaller plane to the island of Crete. Landing on Crete, I found myself on the tarmac by myself and my luggage. I didn't know what to do, but I saw this little guy from far off coming my way. He walked up to me, took my suitcase, and walked off with it. Then he stopped and yelled, "*Ella!*"

What did that mean? He took the suitcases and walked a little farther. He stopped again, turned around, and yelled, "*Ella tho!*"

So I followed him. After all, he did have my luggage. I found out later that *Ella tho* means "Come here." He led me to the main terminal, and I met the agent there. He could speak good English. They both knew more than I did about what was going on, and so I was off to the airbase. Everything was okay. I got checked in and was given a class A pass to get on and off the base. I could now come and go as I pleased as long as I was on duty when I was supposed to be, just like a job back home. Nice duty. It was like going on vacation at the government's expense.

The first two episodes involved being on the job. We had a young kid from, of all places, New York City. He wasn't the brightest light on the block. He would wear his t-shirts until the front got really dirty, then he would turn them around so he had a clean front again. It didn't matter what the back looked like. That wasn't all.

When both the front and the back were dirty, he would pull his shirt off and turn it inside out. Now he had a clean shirt front and back. Was that cool or what? *No!*

One time, the sarge put him on a pallet and lifted him up on the forklift to do some overhead work. About a foot off the ground, the sarge yells at him, "Now, son, don't step off to the side of the pallet or you will fall."

The kid stepped over to the edge of the pallet and said, "What?" just before he fell on the floor. They hauled him away, and somebody else went up on the pallet. Probably me.

The second time, the sarge sent him out to find some invisible paint for the warehouse. The poor boy looked all over the base but couldn't find any. Everybody got a good laugh when the sarge said, "Of course you couldn't find any, it's invisible."

Finally, the sarge sent him out to find a warehouse stretcher. He told him he needed more room in there for the next big shipment. The kid didn't find that either, and we made do with our small warehouse.

New story. There was a long narrow field across the street from the warehouse, and the Greek military used it for mortar practice sometimes. We had an office worker who had just transferred from Vietnam. He came out to the warehouse and jumped on a forklift to get some merchandise. The Greeks fired off a couple of mortars, he jumped off the forklift and spread eagled on the floor (he couldn't have gotten much flatter to the floor). Meanwhile, the forklift was busy going on down the aisle all alone. It hit one freestanding bin row which fell like a domino into another until we had four freestanding bin rows down with tons of electronic parts all over the warehouse. As it turned out, he had been hit in the heels with shrapnel while in Vietnam, and that's why he bailed off the forklift. They still wouldn't let him on a forklift again.

OFF BASE!

We had a driver for the fuel truck. His only job was to make sure the heating fuel and whatever else he had to deliver made its way to those who lived off base. Well, he would take this semitruck right through the town square. The square had a small hut in the middle of it where the officer on duty would direct traffic.

They didn't mind him coming through town until he clipped the hut with the back of his trailer. The hut tipped over, and the traffic cop spilled out like someone pushed him out the door. Our driver watched all this in his rearview mirror, but he didn't stop. All he saw was one mad cop shaking his fist and yelling bad language at him as he went around the next corner. Everybody on base heard about it, and the incident was smoothed over. An apology was sent. Damage corrected.

This same driver who was a friend of mine made another mistake while he was there (two in a year and one half is not bad at all). We were not allowed to share our cigarettes with the locals. He broke the rule one time and was found out. The lieutenant called him on the carpet and dressed him down. In my friend's defense, he said it was an oversight on his part, and if the lieutenant got too cranky with him, he might have memory loss come winter and forget where he lived. The lieutenant let him go!

SHAME ON ME

Several of us would spend weekends off base at the beaches around the island. We all had been drinking during the day, and so when nightfall came, we just kind of crashed in the sand where we landed. Come morning, the sarge said, "Who stepped on me last night?" Everybody looked around, and someone said, "It must have been wisdom."

He was not where he started. It seems I walked in my sleep sometimes. All was well that ends well.

Another time, we were all drinking on base at the sarge's house. I am normally quiet, but when I get to drinking, I often became a motor mouth (always running). I was talking up a storm when in mid-sentence, I stopped, got out of my chair, and went out the door. The sarge had a question. "Where is he going?"

My buddies said, "He is going home to bed."

18

The sarge said, "He didn't even finish his sentence."

They just shrugged their shoulders and said, "We know. He does that all the time."

I got to my barracks and couldn't unlock my door, so around to the back I went and opened my window, crawled in, and fell onto my bed. I woke up the next morning right where I was supposed to be (survived the night again).

SHAME OF SOMEONE ELSE

You guessed it. The group was drinking again. Only thing is there was one among us who hardly ever talked, and he only drank beer. After a while, this is what we heard from him in a loud voice: "Dust bunnies, attention! Forward march! By the left flank, march!"

Around the room he went and back to his chair. He sat down and there was never another word from him that day. He had found all these dust balls on the floor, and he lined them up in a row and marched them around the room. When he got back to his chair, there they were, all lined up where he had left them. *He was a happy camper!*

One among us came from a bad background. He drank every night, but he never got a hangover. Nobody could keep up with him, but one of us tried (not me). We told him he couldn't do it, but you know how young men can be. His answer was, "Sure I can."

At end of day three, he came to us and said, "I can't do this."

We all smiled and said, "We told you so." After that, business as usual.

This same young man that drank all the time ran into trouble one night at the club. He said something to the sergeant in charge that night that he shouldn't. I won't repeat it. This is a family story. The sarge came to us and told us if we got him out of there tonight not to let him come back till the next day. He wouldn't be in the brig in the morning. That is jail, just in case someone hasn't heard the term *brig*. We had just enough people, one for each limb. Two took his legs, and two of us took his arms, and we carried him up the hill to the barracks. Around about 4:00 a.m., he wanted to get up. We wouldn't let him. He begged with us and told us he wouldn't go back down there. It was four in the morning, and we didn't even think that it was closed. We didn't let him up, and he wouldn't talk to us for two weeks. We had begun to wonder if he was ever going to talk to us again. We would say hello when we saw him, but he wouldn't respond. Finally, he opened up to us, and all was well again.

At least one more story from the military chapter. I met this career military man who had maybe ten or fifteen years in, but he only had three stripes. He should have had at least four stripes or more by then. So I asked him about it. He was a drinker, and every time he was stationed stateside, he would get into trouble and lose a stripe. When he was shipped overseas, he would gain it back, and that was the pattern he lived. Kind of sad, but he was okay with it. He never drove a car, and I asked him why. His answer was, "Because I drink."

Well, okay! One more. We had a guy who, of course, drank. Don't most people in the military drink? Anyway, he got drunk and began racing his car all over the base. It took a while for the MPs to corner him. When they did, they took his driver's license and his car away from him. That didn't stop him. He had a bike. He rode his bike to work. He rode his bike off the loading dock at the warehouse. He skinned up his arms, face, and elbows. He got some time off from work for not so good behavior!

3

CIVILIAN AGAIN

Ah! Life after the service. Is it grand or not so grand? First off is to find a new job, which I did. I went to work at a trailer factory. There I worked my tail off (there is that backend again) in the summer and sat on it in the winter. This was not steady work, but while I was there, I managed to shoot my work partner in the head with a T-nail. His head bent the nail. We called him a hard head after that.

I shot myself in the palm of my hand with a panel gun. They called me clumsy after that. I lasted two years there. Next stop was the grocery warehouse. That was more to my liking and my training. I lasted ten years that time. I have many stories from that place.

First, there are lots of food in a grocery warehouse that people like to eat but aren't supposed to. We call that "mousing." Some got pretty good at it, and the supervisors had a tough time catching them at it. The supervisors knew who the culprits were but couldn't prove it. I worked in the deli department where they keep the packaged meats and cheeses and the fresh meats. It stays a constant thirty-three degrees in there twenty-four hours a day, every week. The boss stopped one of the product pullers in the hall outside my little domain and began questioning him. I stepped out to listen. It went something like this.

Boss: I know you are eating. Where is it?
Worker: Where is what?

Boss: Your snacks (as he puts his foot up on the pallet).

Worker: I don't have any snacks.

Boss: I will catch you one of these times, and when I do, I will fire you on the spot.

Bosses like to threaten workers that way. It doesn't work on everybody.

Worker: No, you won't (meaning you will never catch me).

The boss turned and left. I had to ask, so I did.

"Where is it?" I said.

He answered, "It was right under his foot when he was here. You see, the pallet jacks lift up the pallet so they can be moved around the floor. This leaves a space on most of the pallets surface under the jack." The boss never did see it, and he never did catch this young man.

Second. Let's call this man Jim and the warehouse manager. Jim worked in the sundries room. It's a small room and it houses the cigarettes, candies, and spices, small items that everybody would like to get their hands on. Jim had his desk in the middle of the empty space in the room and would walk around it to pull his orders. We received a new warehouse manager, and he thought that process Jim was using was inefficient. He told Jim to move the desk over to the wall. Jim wasn't one to argue, so he said ok.

The manager left, and Jim went back to work. The next day, the manager was back to check on things, and the desk was still in the middle of the floor. He said, "Jim, move that desk over to the wall."

Jim said, "Okay."

The manager left again, and Jim went back to work.

The third day, and the manager came again. The desk was in the middle of the room. The boss said, "If you don't move that desk, I will."

Jim said, "Okay," and the manager moved the desk over to the wall and left. Jim went back to work.

On the fourth day, the manager came in again (he was persistent) but the desk was in the middle of the floor again. Finally, in frustration, the boss said, "To hell with it! Have it your way, Jim!"

Jim said, "Okay." The boss left, Jim went back to work, and nothing changed. That desk was still in the middle of the floor when I left there years later.

Jim was a pretty cool guy. Everybody liked him, even the friends of his teenage children. He also drank some. It seems most people I knew then drank some. It is just the opposite now.

Anyway, this is another story about Jim. We went to the company Christmas party, and every time one of the supervisors came by, they would pat him down. You know, they would slap him on the shoulder, pat his legs, poke at his mid-section all the time, saying, "Hi, Jim, how are you doing? Everything all right with you tonight?"

This went on for a while until I asked him, "What are they doing?"

He responded by saying, "They are looking for my flask."

So I asked a second question. "What happens if they find it?"

He said, "They won't find it."

So I asked again, "Where is it?"

His answer was, "In my boot." He always wore those wellington boots. Then I knew why. The powers that were wanted to sell the alcohol. Jim wasn't about to pay their high prices to drink. By the way, they never did find it.

Later in the night, Jim leaned over to me and said, "Don, you want to go out to the car with me?"

Now this is December and it is cold out there in Idaho in December. I didn't want to go out in the cold, so I told him no.

He said, "Oh! Come on and go out to the car with me."

I say, "Why on earth do I want to go out in the cold with you?"

If you haven't guessed it, here comes his answer. "*My flask is empty!*" Go figure. I am not too bright sometimes. We went out to the car.

One more for good old Jim. From time to time, he would have to come out on the floor and fill orders. One of the ways the company finds out how well the workers are doing is to keep track of how much product you pulled. We were required to pull 150 cases an hour just to stay employed. At the end of the night, Jim's name was always at the top of the list or close to it. He is older, and the young guys are a little bit jealous, but they can't figure out how he does it. They made statements like, "He is old and he looks like he is hardly moving."

It was time for me to explain it to the poor lads. So here it was. "When we pick up a case of groceries and place it on the pallet, we may move it more than once because if you don't do it right, the next corner you go around the stuff just falls off. You have to learn how to stack the pallet so the cases tie together and is solid. Jim, on the other hand, handles a given case only once and moves on to the next product. We work three times as hard and long to get the same thing he gets done in one move. Experience counts."

It's now time to hear from Bruce. Bruce was a little older than me, but not near Jim's age. First story: Yes, Bruce drank some also. One weekend night, he was out and indulged too much. After trying to drive home, he soon realized he had too much to drink. He parked his truck and laid down in the seat and took a nap. That sounds good doesn't it? When he woke up, he was handcuffed to the steering wheel and greeted by the local police. They arrested him and charged him with drunk driving. His day in court came, and his lawyer won his case for him. When he was arrested, he wasn't driving. The only thing is he parked his truck in the middle of the road. It cost him 2,000 dollars to win, but he didn't have a drunk driving charge on his record and he didn't have to go to those classes they require, all because of a technicality.

MORE FROM THE WAREHOUSE!

By the way. None of these stories are in any order. I write them as I remember them. Just thought I would tell you in case you noticed.

Firecracker month. Fourth of July is coming up soon. Firecrackers were not allowed in warehouse. Bosses didn't like them. They showed up anyway. That would show those bosses. Who did they think they were anyway? One of them found its way on to the top of my second pallet. It conveniently landed on a package of powdered Jell-O. When it exploded, there was Jell-O all over me and everything else within two feet around me. No one knew who did it when the boss asked us. Sometimes we aren't too smart. We just couldn't figure out who did such a crime. No help at all for the boss. He wasn't happy, but we were.

This is one of my favorite stories. Are you ready for this? Here it comes, ready or not. We have this PA system we used to call in what was called a breakdown. The warehouse had picking bays at ground floor and overstock bays the next row up and at the very top. When the picking bay became empty, we found a speaker and called in to have a forklift come and put a pallet on the floor where we could reach it. Workers came and went in an operation like that, and they had a big turnover of people. One day, every now and again, we would hear over the PA "Ribbit! ribbit!" Like a frog. You know the sound. I know you do!

The production supervisor got tired of it, so we had a meeting. Production stopped! We heard this: "Whoever is playing frog on the PA had better stop it *now*! If I catch you at it, you are fired on the spot. Now get back to work, and no more playing around." Well, folks, I didn't even get back to my pallet jack when I heard "Ribbit! Ribbit!" The whole warehouse broke out in laughter.

Sometimes we would get damaged goods, and some of it would find its way into the trash bin outside. Not supposed to, but it did anyway. There was this guy living on the streets in the dumpster, looking for whatever he could find. The powers who were found him out there, and they told him to get out of there. His response? No.

"We will call the police if you don't."

Response? "Go ahead."

They did. The police came and put him in the car to haul him away to jail. Now winter Was about to show up, so the homeless guy yelled out the window of the police car, "Thanks, I needed a home for the winter!" He waved at us as he went down the street.

That reminds me of one of my uncles. He didn't pay his child support and found himself without funds. Once again, winter was coming. This is what he did: He came to Boise, marched up to his ex-wife's house, and knocked on her door. She opened, and he said, "Hi! Here I am."

She slammed the door and called the police. He sat on the doorstep and waited. They came. They left with him in tow. He spent the winter in jail, playing poker with the other inmates. Spring came. He left with money in his pockets. It was a good winter.

BACK TO THE WAREHOUSE

Remember that guy that got arrested for drunk driving.? This time, he was working out on the front dock in the warehouse. He found this knot, picked it up, and threw it at the warehouse foreman. He didn't think he would ever hit him, but guess what? He did—right in the back of the head. "Everybody, duck down like right now!"

The foreman looked around, and nobody was out there. Once again, we weren't too bright. When the questions came, nobody knew anything or saw anything. Sometimes I would feel sorry for management in the warehouse. *Not!*

I had the privilege of working up the frozen turkey orders during October and November. My crew and I would work till three or four or five in the morning to get our job done. After about three weeks of this, I began to have dreams. Picture this: News headline: "Frozen turkeys escape their boxes and hunt down local warehouse worker." It's a wonder I didn't have a heart attack from those dreams. Even now, I don't like looking at frozen turkeys. I won't go down the meat aisle. Okay, just kidding. I am a well-adjusted old fuddy-duddy.

THE FAMILY!

Now I got me a story that is a little different. My dad was one of seven boys. That's a lot of uncles. My brother and me—or is it my brother and I?—went to one of the uncles houses one day and was talking to him. We asked him why he never got married. He just said, "I drink." He may never have had a wife, but he did have a dog.

Two matters of fact, not at the same time. Nobody has two dogs at the same time. Do they? Anyway, he said, "You boys want to see something interesting?"

"Sure," we said.

He said, "Take my whiskey bottle and go hide it somewhere in the house. Not to high up but down where this here dog can find it."

"Okay." So we did.

When we came back, he said, "Did you hide it good?"

We answered, "Yes." We hid it in the pantry around the food.

He called his dog over and said, "Fetch my bottle." That dog wasn't gone over a few piddlin' moments when here he comes with the bottle in his mouth. We didn't know dogs could sniff like that. I thought he just read our minds. Well, mine anyway. I don't think brother ever had one.

Maybe the dog heard us talking. Dogs understand all languages you know.

That's not all he could do. Uncle said, "Now watch this." He took a drink out the bottle, put a cigarette in his mouth, lit it, and then lay down on the bed and began to snore. After a few moments, he let his hand fall off the side of the bed and let the cigarette hit the floor.

On cue, the dog jumped up, and with one of his big paws (he was right-handed because that's the paw he used) and went *pat, pat, pat* on the cigarette until it was put out. Then Uncle asked us, "Why would I need a wife?"

One of our other uncles and my brother went fishing up on the north fork of the Boise River. I think it was there anyway. They were fishing and waiting for some action when our uncle said this: "A couple of months ago, I was up here fishing all by myself when I hooked and landed the biggest trout I ever landed, and you know what? When I opened him up to clean him, I found an old oil lantern inside there, and it was still lit."

My brother, not wanting to be out told, said, "That is nothing. I was up two weeks ago and was fishing along, minding my own business, when I heard this really deep growling sound. The longer I listened, the louder it got. It was right behind me in the air. I looked up, and there was this jet plane about to crash in that mountain. You know what that pilot did? Well, he stomped on the air brakes, put that plane in reverse, backed up, pointed the plane toward the sky, and flew over the top of that mountain."

My uncle said, "I don't believe that for one minute."

My brother said, "I'll tell you what. You blow out that lantern, and I will let that plane crash into the mountain."

THE FIRST LIAR NEVER HAS A CHANCE!

How about a cousin story? I don't like to use names here for fear of repercussions. So here goes. The wife, bless her soul, sent my cousin out to get a loaf of bread. It seems he went on a walkabout, for it took about six months to find his way back. Now in defense of my cousin, he did bring back a fresh loaf of bread. She took the bread and went about her business as if nothing happened. They have been together now for I don't know how many years—forty or more. He never strayed again.

They lived happily ever after!

THE MACHINE SHOP

What can I say about the machine shop? I know there are stories there. There has to be after ten years there. My job was shipping, receiving, warehousing, and chasing parts. We had a mechanic shop supervisor who liked to test people, especially the new guys like me. Here he came one day through the warehouse, and he stopped and said, "Don, run over to Kaman Bearing. Pick up an order for me."

I said, "No."

He said, "Why not?"

I said, "Because I don't work for you."

My boss was the purchasing agent. He got angry and said, "We will see about that. I will go talk to the general manager (the big boss)."

I said, "Fine, I'll go with you." He turned around and walks out the door he came in. Didn't even make to the office.

Another time, same mechanic boss, same problem. I wouldn't do what he wanted. He threatened to kick my backside (notice how that backside keeps coming into the picture). I just said, "Fine, but I still won't go get your part."

There he went out the door he came in. I went back to work.

One more time with this guy. Five o' clock, we went home for the day. Here he came. "Run over to Kaman Bearing and get this part."

Once again, I said, "No. If you want it, you go get it."

He said, "No, tomorrow will be okay. I don't need it till the morning."

Next up, the machine shop supervisor. He seemed to be gone a lot. You could never find him when you needed him. When supplies came in, we couldn't distribute to the different areas where they belonged. So we just put them wherever we could find a spot. He didn't like that, so he complained and let us know that we were looking him up when we had something for him. He wouldn't make a staging area for us. My coworker and I received about a five-foot piece of cold roll with a diameter of maybe six inches. This is a heavy piece of round metal solid. It took two of us to load it in the pickup and take it up to the machine shop. You guessed it. He wasn't anywhere to be found, so we unloaded it onto his chair in his office. He should be able to find it, don't you think? He did!

He called the office, yelled at the assistant purchasing agent, blamed me and my coworker whose idea it was to use the chair, and we got away scot-free. You want to know what my boss had to say. Here it comes: "Well, he could find it, couldn't he?" End of story.

My boss sent me out to get some parts, and one of the stops usually gave out a hat for advertising. One hat, and four department heads wanted it. What was I to do? I knew I would auction it off to the highest bidder. Guess who got the hat? Go ahead, guess. The winner was *my boss*. He was the only one who could fire me. I know who buttered my bread there.

We had an assistant purchasing agent who was kind of a ladies' man. He decided to date three women at the same time (notice I didn't say he was smart). I wandered up to the front desk, and there he sat with his head in his hands. I asked, "What's wrong?"

He pointed at this vase of flowers on the counter. Now I'm not too bright sometimes either. He said it was for me but it wasn't signed. Now what does he do? He can't even thank one for the flowers because the odds were against him to get the right one, but if he didn't do anything, someone would wonder why he didn't respond. You will have to decide on your own if he survived that or not.

THE CHILDREN

What do I say about the children? I know that any parent knows there is a difference between raising girls and raising boys. In case you are raising both boys and girls, you know that is another different story indeed. Each has its own trials and pleasures, but whatever we as parents see in our children, the trip is worth it. If we are lucky, we get to see well-adjusted young adults who have stayed out of trouble and found their own path in life. I am happy to say I am one of those parents.

I helped raise four girls, all with different personalities and ideas about life. It was wonderful, even with its challenges. I would like to share some of the memories with you.

The oldest, Naomie, was a challenge. She wasn't a rabble-rouser, but she did think different than most people do. Her moral compass was a little lax. She didn't do things on purpose to get in trouble. It just seemed to happen. For instance, in grade school, she and another little boy were acting up in class when they should have been listening. The teacher made them stay in class when all the children went outside for recess. It was a special day, and there were cookies there for everyone to eat later. If you haven't guessed yet, those two little angels sat there and ate every single one of them. I am sure they weren't the most popular kids in school that day.

We had a parent-teacher meeting not long after that, and the teacher informed us, "She isn't a bad kid, she just doesn't make good decisions." However, she made it through school and life without serious trouble. She left home as a teenager and got married.

The second child, Henryetta, her biggest problem was boys. For that matter, both of the older girls were in that boat.

Their problems were also our problems. As in many marriages nowadays, my wife and I divorced. The girls stayed with Mom, and I would come over after work and stay with them so their mom could go to work. Sometimes I would fall asleep in the easy chair. That was when Henryetta would sneak out and go run around with the boys. I hate to admit it, but I never did catch her. She didn't even tell me about it till she was forty some years old. I have many stories from the children, and I can't tell them all, but I will tell you this. Do not roughhouse with teenage girls because they will put you on the floor. I have this bad thumb, and when Henryetta grabbed it, I was on the floor in an instant. None of them let me live that episode down. I did get the last laugh on her. When she got married, I walked up front to give her away and handed her future husband a dollar bill and said, "She is your problem now." Everybody got a good laugh, and I walked away a proud man.

Third child—Michell. What can I say here? Her things were stopping on the way to school and playing with whatever she could find (usually something in the gutter). Again, it was time to talk to a teacher. We asked how she was doing. Her answer? "Fine, when she is here." She told us she would come in an hour or two late sometimes. So we talked to her older sisters and made it clear that they got her there on time.

Sometimes I think we spent more time in school than they did. Michell liked to catch grasshoppers, lean up against the garage wall, and feed them one blade of grass at a time. It seems she liked to see them nibble on the grass. She turned out to be the most mouthy one. They are all adults now, and she is the hardest one to stay ahead of when we banter verbally. Michell's husband can hold his own with her and anybody else, but when it comes to dealing with the car salesmen, he lets her go to work. They can't get around her. She gets what she wants at the price she wants or they don't get a sale. She walks off, leaving them there, dumbfounded.

Here is an example. About the third or fourth car lot, she found the car she wanted but she didn't like the radio. She liked the radio in another car. The salesman got sneaky, but it didn't work. He said, "You telling me you won't buy this car without that radio in it?"

She said, "You telling me you are willing to lose a sale because of a radio?" She also told him, "I will buy this car if you put that radio in it."

His response? "Just a minute." He talked to his boss. She got the car she wanted at the price she would pay with the radio she wanted. She was happy. His boss was happy. I don't know about the salesman, but he learned a lesson.

Fourth child. She is a peacekeeper. She has a mild, gentle personality—soft-spoken, easy to get along with for the most part. They all had chores to do, so this is what you would hear: "I did the dishes last week, it's your turn." While the others were facing off to see who should be doing dishes, she would go in and wash dishes. It seemed everybody was happy with that arrangement. Even though she was mild-mannered, she wasn't a pushover. She has had some boyfriends who didn't treat her right, so she told them to pack up and get out, and they did. What they didn't know was that if they didn't leave, I would help her. They all knew I would be there to convert anybody. I just wanted to follow through with my life pattern.

My third wife and the most wonderful woman I have ever known wanted to go back to church. She fretted and worried about two weeks before talking to me about it, but I surprised her. I said, "I will go with you." At this point, I knew nothing about being faith-based. I didn't grow up knowing God. First week, we got up, got dressed, and backed out. We didn't go. Second week—a repeat of the first. Third week, we talked about it and decided to force the issue or we wouldn't ever go, so we got up, got dressed, and we were on our way. Into the church we went and straight to the back pew where we thought we wouldn't be noticed. That didn't work well. As soon as you walk in the door, everybody sees new blood.

Our plan was to slip out the door quickly after the sermon. That didn't work. It seems you file from the front pews to the back when it is time to leave. We were the last ones to get up. Fast-forward a little bit. I began to notice only a few members seemed to be doing most of the work. This didn't seem right to me. Sometimes we had a short video at the beginning of the services, so I got up and started closing the blinds. That was a mistake or not, depending on how you looked at it. I wanted to help, and now I was part of the church family. A short time later, the pastor asked me if I would like to be a deacon.

Now I don't even know what a deacon is, and I told him so. That didn't bother him. He gave me some scripture to read. When I read it, I found out you are be honest and upright and dependable and have only one wife. This was my way out, I think. I went back to the pastor and told him I couldn't be a deacon because I had been married three times. Good excuse, don't you think? Again, he was not worried, so he said, "You only married one at a time."

I became a deacon. Now I had all the work I cared to have. For those of you who might not know, one of the deacon's jobs is to fix things when they get broke. More time goes by, and I was asked to see if I would like to teach the lesson one week of the month. We had lesson studies before we even got to the sermon time frame. The man that asked me was one of the elders. This was what he said: "I have been teaching the lessons every week for the past forty years, and I am getting tired. Would you be willing to help?"

Again, I had an answer. "These people have forgotten more than I will ever know. It would be like preaching to the pastor."

But again, he had an answer. "The lessons are in a book, and he says all you have to do is read it and present in your own words."

There was a lesson here for me. I had to learn how to say no! That was lesson I had never learned. I was now an elder up on the podium. To this day, I struggle through that process. But enough of this. I want to share some stories with you.

We had some greenery planted too close to the building and we there to remove it. Now we had a lady who was strong-willed and really didn't want us to do that. Picture this. Four or five big strong men working on the project when someone asked, "Does Jill know what we are doing?"

The head elder answered with a voice that didn't sound too convincing, "I am not afraid of Jill."

"I am not afraid of Jill either, but that isn't her real name." We got the job done and survived it. By the way, Jill planted flowers where the greenery was. No one challenged her.

Next story. Now we had our second head elder since I had been there. He was a building contractor on his way to a jobsite. He was pulling a flatbed trailer with a backhoe on it when something didn't feel right there. He found a big wide place to pull over on. He got out and walked back to the trailer in the gravel and jumped up on the trailer to see what he could find. The boom on the trailer swung loose and knocked him off into the gravel. This knocked him out. He woke up hours later in the hospital fifty miles away in Boise, Idaho. He was questioned about what happened and he told them. He didn't remember anything, so it was his turn to ask. "How did I get here?"

They old him, "A big tall man carried you." And they told him how he found him. They got busy with his care, and the tall man was gone. Once our elder remembered things, he told them where the truck was, and the police investigated. They found the truck in this big wide graveled area. What they didn't find was any tire tracks entering the graveled area but his truck tires. They didn't find footprints but his. They didn't find where someone jumped up or down off the trailer. The gravel had been undisturbed.

The people at the hospital couldn't describe the man who brought him in. All they could tell the police was that he carried him in, and when they turned around, he was gone. The rest of the story is up to you.

The next story is one I read. I hope I don't get in trouble for rewriting it. This young lady worked the swing shift. It was dark when she walked home from work. We were in a city here, and she was walking down a sidewalk. The street was on one side of her, and a block wall was on the other. There were streetlights spaced along there also so she would walk in and out of the shadows. She could see this man ahead of her, leaning against the wall. This made her a bit nervous, to say the least, but she walked on anyway. She managed to walk by him, and he didn't even move.

Maybe two days later, she read a news story about a man who was arrested for attacking a woman on that same sidewalk. She told the police her story about him, and they asked him, "Why didn't you attack the woman that was there two days earlier?"

34

This was his response: "She had very big escorts with her, one on each side." She said she was alone that night. People who saw her walking before and after that part of her walk never saw anyone with her. End of story.

I am older now, and things begin to happen with age. You older folks will know about this. It even happens to younger people who have busy lives. We misplace things. I lost my glasses once, so I looked in the back bedroom, in the front bedroom, in the kitchen, and living room. I looked in the dining room, in the bathroom, and I even went outside to look in the car. I finally found them. They were hanging off the bridge of my nose. Sometimes one can get so used to something, you don't know you have it. So I lost my billfold in my pocket, my keys in my pocket and in the door of my car, gloves in my coat, cell phone lying on the counter in front of me. Oh, but it makes life interesting, doesn't it? Please don't forget where you left your wife or husband. That could be a problem. When we get up in the morning, we should remember to put our pants on. If we don't remember, that will be the day someone stopped by to see how we are doing.

We seem to gather things as we age. I have four pairs of pants, four long-sleeved sweaters, six pullover shirts, six dress shirts, which I only wear to church, five pairs of slacks, which I only wear two— and that's only one at a time—six white t-shirts, seven t-shirts with various saying and pictures on them, twelve pairs of socks, five coats, and a pair of snow coveralls with snow boots. I have a three-cushion couch with recliners on each end, a two-cushion couch with recliners, two single recliners, and I am the only one in the house. I have a TV, a computer, and a Wii game console to keep me busy. I think you get the picture.

DONKEY BASEBALL

If you have never seen a game of donkey baseball, you have missed a real treat. You will need two teams of nine players each and six donkeys. All the donkeys will have a harness on so the riders have a way to control the animals (that won't happen). In addition, the outfielders will have a long rope attached to their donkey. They will need to be able to jump off the donkey to chase a ball.

Scene one—batter up. The ball is hit. He jumps on the donkey and heads for first base. The outfielder jumps off his donkey and heads for the ball. He is required to stay attached to his rope. So he runs for the ball and it rolls out of reach, and the outfielder is upended. Now he tugs on the rope, trying to get the donkey to move so he can get the ball that is just sitting there now. He can't reach it, but all is not lost. The runner going for first base has lost control of his donkey. It stops, and he is pitched over the donkey's head into the outfield. He has to get back on the donkey, and the outfielder has to get the ball. Nothing happens.

The runner at first base is safe. Batter up! Second batter hit's the ball, and he is headed for first base. First batter rides to second base. The donkey doesn't want to go, but he gets him there, finally. Third batter hits the ball, and he is off to first base. First batter is off to third base. Second batter is off to second base. Third batter doesn't get to first base. The donkey just stops and refuses to go any farther. He probes him to get him there, and the bases are loaded.

Fourth batter strikes out. The donkey on third runs for home base and scores. Meanwhile, the donkey on second base refuses to run. The donkey on first base runs to second base, and now you have two on second base. You can't have that, and we get a total traffic jam. The player to hit the ball hasn't made it first base because the donkey refuses to move. Meanwhile, the fans sides are beginning to hurt from all the laughing. The point of this story is if you get the chance to watch donkey baseball, do it. You won't be sorry.

JUST STUFF SECTION

I thought I would put whatever came to mind whenever it came to mind in this last section. As you guys all know, when it comes to the women folk, you need to be careful of what you do sometimes. Case in point: I had this silver dollar that we were tossing around when it got away from us and rolled somewhere out of sight. So we were down on our knees, looking for it. We looked for a while when I finally found it. I just palmed it in my hand and pretended to keep hunting.

After a bit, I faked my knees were hurting, so I sat on a couch and watched her crawl around on the floor, looking for the dollar. Finally, I said, "Oh, here it is."

Question: "Where was it?"

Mistake: "Oh, I found it right there by the end table five minutes ago."

I liked not to survive that episode. Some of us guys should learn to think before we talk. That is a lesson I haven't learned yet!

ABOUT THE AUTHOR

This is Don Wisdom's first book. After retirement, he needed something to do, so he began to write about things that happened as he traveled through life. Somewhere along the line, he thought he might be able to make a book out it. This is that book.